BIRDSONG LULLABY

BIRDSONG LULLABY

Story and pictures by DIANE STANLEY

William Morrow and Company, Inc., New York

For Nora Cohen

Library of Congress Cataloging in Publication Data
Stanley, Diane.   Birdsong lullaby.
Summary: A little girl imagines all the things she could do if she were a bird. 1. Children's stories,
American. [1. Birds—Fiction] I. Title.   PZ7.S7869Bi   1985   [E]   85-5654
ISBN 0-688-05804-3
ISBN 0-688-05805-1 (lib. bdg.)

"Momma?" asked the little girl.

"Yes," her mother said.

"I was thinking…"

"What were you thinking, dearest?"

"If I were a bird…"

"...if I were a bird,
   I could fly anywhere I wanted
   and see such wonderful things!"

"Really? What would you like to see?"

"If I were a bird,
I could sit on people's windowsills
and peek inside their houses."

"That's right. You could."

"I could play in our birdbath."
"And I'd bring you sunflower seeds to eat."
"No, cake!"
"All right then, cake."

"If I were a bird,
   I could look down into people's backyards…"

"I could catch all
the lost balloons
and give them back
to children."

"What a pretty idea!"

"If I were a bird,
  I could see what kind
  of pajamas kings wear."

"When it got cold,
  I could go to Brazil
  and live in a tree full of monkeys."

"And you'd tuck your head
  under your wing to sleep."

"In the summer,
    I'd fly to the seashore
    and play with the waves."

"Or look down
over mountain lakes
and see my reflection."

"If I were a bird,
I could soar through the air,
then land gently
and not hurt myself at all.
I could float on the wind
and touch the clouds!"

"And, Momma—I could fly right into a rainbow
and come out full of colors…"

"Maybe you'll dream about it tonight."

"You think so, Momma?"

"And it will seem *so real*…"

"It *will* be real!"

"Yes, darling."

"Momma…"

"*Shhh,* go to sleep."

"Momma?"

"What, sweet?"

"Leave my window open tonight…"